Protoceratops

Protoceratops

Heather Amery

Illustrated by Tony Gibbons

PARRAGON

Contents

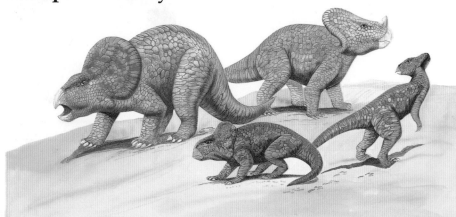

Introducing
Protoceratops

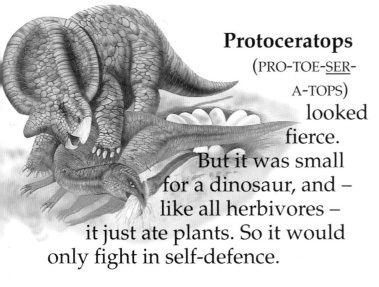

Protoceratops (PRO-TOE-<u>SER</u>-A-TOPS) looked fierce. But it was small for a dinosaur, and – like all herbivores – it just ate plants. So it would only fight in self-defence.

This dinosaur lived millions of years ago in Late Cretaceous times, wandering about in peaceful herds of several families, and feeding on tough, woody plants. The females laid eggs, guarding them until they hatched.

Scientists know from its skeleton that **Protoceratops** had a beaked mouth, rather like a turtle's, and a large bony frill around the back of its neck.

With a heavy, clumsy body, it stumped along on four sturdy legs, holding up its thick tail.

Where did scientists first find **Protoceratops?** How did it look after its eggs? What do we now know about this strange creature?

Could **Protoceratops** fight off the meat-eating dinosaurs? Did it use the frill around its neck as a weapon, or was this just for show?

Read about one of the most interesting dinosaurs of all as you turn the pages that follow.

Frilled creature

Protoceratops was a squat, clumsy-looking dinosaur which lived in what is now the Gobi desert in Mongolia, Asia.

About as long as a bed and only as high as your waist, it plodded along on four stumpy legs.

It had a big head with a bony frill around its neck. This made it look quite fierce and dangerous; and it may well have scared you, if you had suddenly come face-to-face with one. But, of course, there were no humans around about 100 million years ago. And, anyway, it probably did not fight unless attacked.

There were bumps, a bit like horns, on **Protoceratops'** head. But these were really tiny when compared with the much larger horns of such dinosaurs as **Triceratops** (TRY-<u>SER</u>-A-TOPS).

6

Protoceratops bit off vegetation with its horn-covered beak, which was curved like a parrot's. Then it crunched up its food between the rows of short, blunt teeth at the back of its jaws.

Although Protoceratops had no teeth at the front of its mouth, it could have given an enemy a nasty nip with its beak.

Its enemies were large meat-eaters like Tarbosaurus (TAR-BO-SAW-RUS), who thought it would make a good meal.

Another tool for putting up a fight against predators was Protoceratops' large, thick tail. This was almost as long as its body. It may have used the tail to whack at its enemies, giving violent sideways blows. This would have wounded the enemy and stopped their attack.

Protoceratops' head frill would also have been useful in times of danger, protecting its body, rather like a shield.

The frill provided an anchor for strong jaw muscles, too. But it was not as heavy as it looks because there were large openings in the bone at its back edge.

Adult males probably had frills that were more upright than those of female Protoceratops, scientists believe. The males also may have had more prominent snouts. These larger frills and snouts may have made the males more attractive to females.

7

Small but powerful

Protoceratops had a skeleton of strong, thick bone to hold up the weight of its bulky body, which was heavy for its small size. Most Protoceratops were no bigger than large dogs.

Scientists think that Protoceratops walked mainly on all-fours. But it may have been able to balance on its hind legs.

Notice how the back legs of Protoceratops were much longer than the front ones.

Protoceratops could probably run quite fast when in danger, but it was usually content to lumber along.

The skeletons of the males were probably much larger than those of the females. **Protoceratops** skeletons also seem to have had differently shaped frills around their necks. Frills belonging to the males were probably bigger, too, just as their bodies were.

Take a look at the size of **Protoceratops'** head. It was about half the length of its body, without the tail.

There were no teeth at the front of the beak, which was made of hard bone.

Protoceratops' jaws had strong muscles that helped it chew at plants. It also had powerful muscles linked to the neck frill which were used for holding up its head. As it moved, **Protoceratops** held its head up level with its body and tail.

The frill was like a round, flat collar, and was made of solid bone. It spread out backwards from its skull. The bone had two large holes in it, to make it lighter.

Thousands of years ago, when the Chinese found bones and teeth like those of this skeleton, they thought they belonged to dragons.

Protoceratops had a curious mouth, shaped like a curved beak. The top jaw was longer than the lower jaw.

But, of course, dragons never really existed. We now know that they were the bones of dinosaurs such as **Protoceratops.**

Protoceratops discovered

About 70 years ago, a group of scientists from the American Museum of Natural History went on an expedition to the Gobi desert of Mongolia.

They were hoping to find proof that the first human beings had lived there and to learn something about them.

After many months of exploration, the scientists found nothing. Then, suddenly, they made a very different and exciting discovery.

In an area that is called Flaming Cliffs, because of the red colour of its rocks, the explorers came across many fossilized dinosaur nests, filled with eggs – the first that had ever been found.

Near the nests were lots of bones that seemed to come from a strange dinosaur with a frill around its neck. They named it **Protoceratops.**

They also found the fossilized bones of tiny, newly-hatched dinosaurs, babies still in the eggs, and hundreds of pieces of egg shell.

The scientists, by accident, had stumbled across something very special – the first dinosaur eggs ever to be found.

Until this discovery, scientists had not known whether dinosaurs hatched out of eggs, like reptiles, or if the young were born alive.

Life with Protoceratops

Protoceratops lived in family groups in the Gobi desert, in Mongolia.

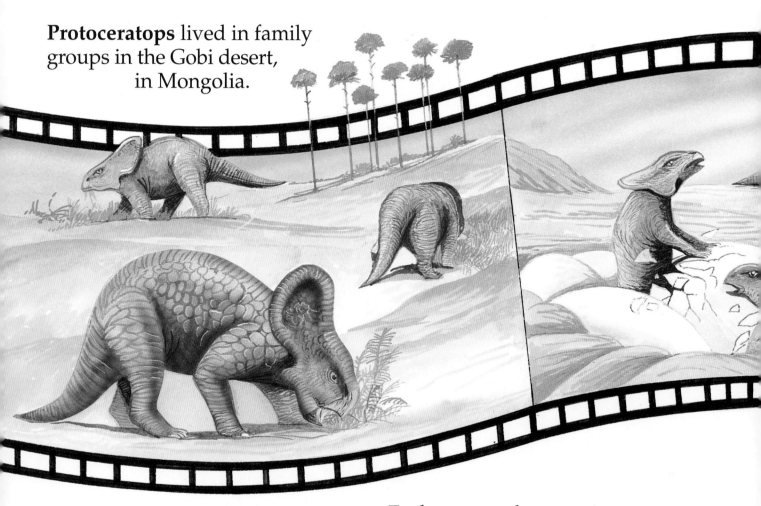

Millions of years ago, the weather was warm with no cold winters, and the plants and trees grew quickly.

Each year, at the beginning of the mating season, the males in each **Protoceratops** herd fought each other for females. Then they would mate.

The females laid eggs. Once the young had hatched out, the females guarded them. Later, when the babies were old enough, the herd may have moved on together to find fresh feeding grounds.

There were giant, meat-eating dinosaurs which would attack **Protoceratops**, too. **Tarbosaurus**, for example, was as long as three cars and nearly as tall as a giraffe.

Tarbosaurus had a huge mouth with long, sharp teeth. Even the biggest and strongest **Protoceratops** was no match for this huge predator.

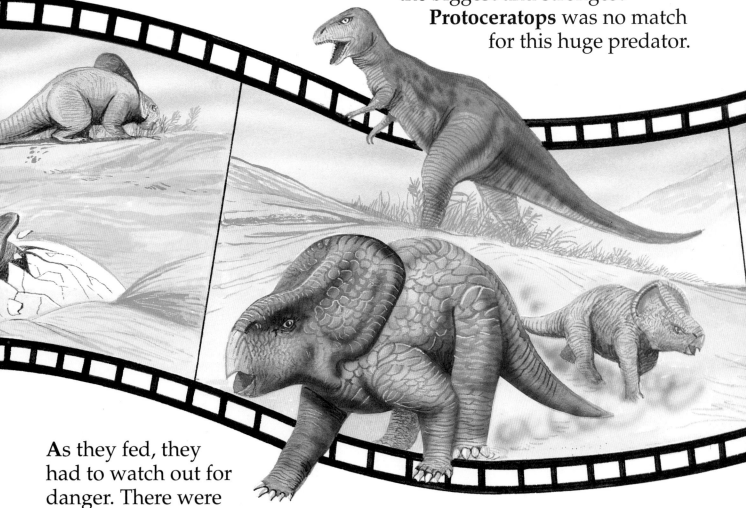

As they fed, they had to watch out for danger. There were many small dinosaurs which would try to steal **Protoceratops'** eggs or snatch a baby.

This is why it was important for **Protoceratops** to stay together in the herd.

13

Leader of the pack

Herds of Protoceratops roamed the plains of Mongolia, in Asia, about 100 million years ago.

Like herds of deer or elephants today, they lived in peaceful family groups for most of the year.

But at the start of the mating season, scientists think that a young male would challenge the old leader to see who would lead the herd next.

Standing a few metres apart, they would roar fiercely at one another. Then they charged – butting each other with their bony heads, giving powerful sideways blows with their frills and whacking their tails.

The battle could last just for a few minutes or much longer.

When, at last, the weaker one gave in to the stronger one, it walked away. It may have been battered and bruised but was probably not seriously wounded. It now took its place in the herd again until the next mating season began. The victor would be the new leader of the herd.

Dinosaur nursery

Near Flaming Cliffs in the Gobi desert, a herd of **Protoceratops** stopped to lay their eggs. The mothers used their feet to scrape out round nests, like shallow basins, in the sandy soil.

When a nest was ready, a mother would carefully drop each egg, starting in the middle of the nest and moving slowly round, in a neat spiral. When she had laid about 12 eggs, the mother plodded away to leave room for another mother to lay her eggs in the same, shared nest. The eggs of several mothers would therefore hatch from one nest.

16

Nearby there would have been other **Protoceratops** nests, with up to 30 eggs in each. **Protoceratops** mothers probably covered their eggs with sand to keep them warm.

Instead of sitting on the nests, they relied on the sun's heat to incubate the eggs. The eggs were about 20 cm long and shaped like fat sausages. The tough, wrinkly shells protected the growing babies, curled up inside, from being crushed or drying out.

When the baby **Protoceratops** hatched out of their shells, they were only about 30 cm long.

The mothers probably brought them food and guarded them against such meat-eating (carnivore) dinosaurs as **Tarbosaurus.**

Soon, they would be old and strong enough to look after themselves.

Many **Protoceratops** nests that have been found are very well preserved.

On guard!

A Protoceratops mother lay on the sandy ground, resting by her nest in the heat of the day. The sun was helping to incubate her eggs. They would soon hatch.

But there were dinosaur egg-thieves about who might possibly steal and eat them.

Oviraptor (<u>OVE</u>-IH-<u>RAP</u>-TOR), for instance, was a small dinosaur with strong three-fingered hands. Its name means 'egg-stealer'. It had strong jaws and a bony beak that could easily crack a shell, even though it had no teeth.

But **Oviraptor** would have thought twice about attacking an adult **Protoceratops**. This dinosaur had such a tough, well-armoured body that **Oviraptor** would have stood little chance of hurting it. **Oviraptor** knew that its best chance of having a dinosaur for dinner was if it could gets its hands on a baby, or steal some eggs.

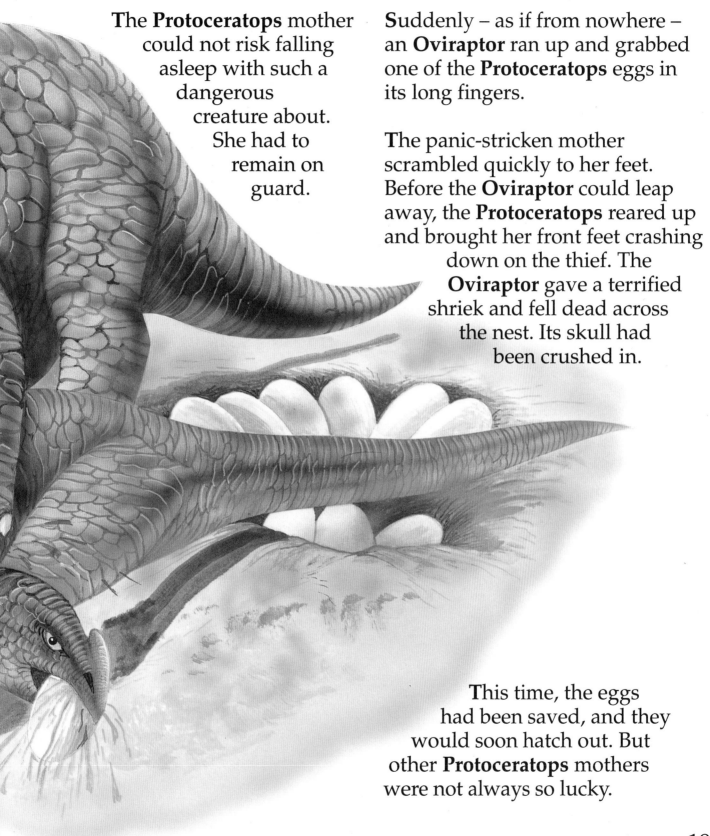

The **Protoceratops** mother could not risk falling asleep with such a dangerous creature about. She had to remain on guard.

Suddenly – as if from nowhere – an **Oviraptor** ran up and grabbed one of the **Protoceratops** eggs in its long fingers.

The panic-stricken mother scrambled quickly to her feet. Before the **Oviraptor** could leap away, the **Protoceratops** reared up and brought her front feet crashing down on the thief. The **Oviraptor** gave a terrified shriek and fell dead across the nest. Its skull had been crushed in.

This time, the eggs had been saved, and they would soon hatch out. But other **Protoceratops** mothers were not always so lucky.

Protoceratops data

Protoceratops was a small, bulky dinosaur. It had a big head with a frilly collar and a bumpy snout. Walking heavily on all four legs, it probably swayed its thick tail from side to side as it searched for fresh plants to eat.

Parrot-beak

Protoceratops had no teeth at the front of its mouth. Instead, it had a bony beak, shaped very much like a parrot's. At the back of its jaws, it had rows of teeth for grinding up all the tough leaves and plants that it plucked off with its beak.

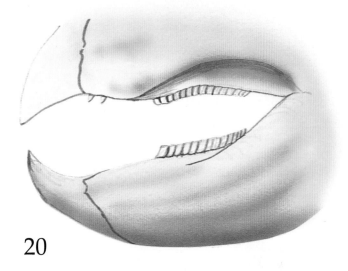

Frilly collar

Protoceratops had a big bony frill around its neck. This acted like a shield, protecting it from the claws and teeth of the meat-eating dinosaurs which attacked it. The frills of the males may have been bigger than those of females. They may also have used their frills to signal to the rest of the herd at the start of the mating season.

Bony head

Protoceratops had a big, heavy head with bony bumps on its nose, rather like small, lumpy horns. It also had bumps over its eyes. Scientists think that **Protoceratops** must have used its strong skull for butting and pushing other members of its herd, when fighting for leadership.

Clawed feet

Protoceratops' feet were broad and strong. There were four toes with short claws on each foot. They were probably too short to be useful for fighting, but they may have helped **Protoceratops** to get a grip on slippery ground. The females would also have used these claws when scraping out their nests.

Thick tail

Almost as long as its body, **Protoceratops'** tail was thick and powerful. It probably held it up when running. A single sideways blow with its tail would have broken the leg of a small attacking dinosaur quite easily. **Protoceratops** may also have used its tail in a swishing movement to ward off a challenge from another male. Notice how the tail tapered towards the end.

The Protoceratopsid family

Protoceratops belonged to a dinosaur family, or group, called **Protoceratopsids.** There were several different branches of this group which lived in different parts of the world. They were small dinosaurs with bony lumps on their noses and frills around their necks.

1

3

Protoceratops (1), with a name meaning 'first horned face', is the earliest known dinosaur to have lumps, like very small horns, on its head. It roamed around in herds, eating plants and trees.

Montanaceratops, (<u>MON</u>-TANNA-<u>SER</u>-A-TOPS) **(2)**, was a cousin of **Protoceratops** and was about twice as long.

Montanaceratops means 'horned face from Montana'.

Bagaceratops, (<u>BAG</u>-A-<u>SER</u>-A-TOPS) **(3)**, was a smaller member of the family. Like the others, it had a neck frill, a parrot-like beak and a nose horn. Its name means 'small horned face'.

Microceratops, (<u>MY</u>-CRO-<u>SER</u>-A-TOPS) **(4)**, was another relative. It is also one of the smallest dinosaurs ever found.

First published 1993
by Parragon Book Service, Bristol

Text and illustrations copyright
© 1993 Quartz Editorial Services
112 Station Road, Edgware HA8 7AQ

ISBN 1–85813–343–2

Printed and bound in Great Britain by BPCC Paulton Books